D0461748

Newfoundland
Water Rescuer

by Dawn Bluemel Oldfield

Consultant: Jim Bricknell
President, Newfoundland Dog Club of Canada

BEARPORT
PUBLISHING

New York, New York

Credits

Cover and Title Page, © CB2/ZOB/WENN/Newscom; TOC, © Eric Isselée/Shutterstock; 4, © Colin Shepherd/ Rex USA/BEImages; 5, © Colin Shepherd/Rex USA/BEImages; 6, © Colin Shepherd/Rex USA/BEImages; 7, © AP Photo/Courtesy of Italian School of Canine Lifeguards; 8, © Timothy Houle; 9, © Pascal Guyot/AFP/Newscom; 10, © Canada Post Corporation 1988. Reproduced with Permission. Library and Archives Canada, 1988, POSTAL 1171; 11T, © katewarn images/Alamy; 11B, © Exactostock/SuperStock; 12, © canadabrian/Alamy; 13, © Robert E. Lougheed/National Geographic/Getty Images; 14, © Newfoundland Dog Called Lion, 1824 (oil on canvas) by Sir Edwin Landseer (1802-73) Victoria & Albert Museum, London, UK/The Stapleton Collection/ The Bridgeman Art Library; 15L, © Phillip Augustavo/Alamy; 15R, © Anne Mainman; 16, © Ashbey Photography; 17, © AP Photo/The Forum/Dave Wallis; 18, © AP Photo/Courtesy of Italian School of Canine Lifeguards; 19T, © Syracuse Newspapers/ David Lassman/The Image Works; 19B, © Kent News/Rex USA/BEImages; 20, © NaturePL/SuperStock; 21, © H. Mark Weidman Photography/Alamy; 22, © Top-Pet-Pics/Alamy; 23L, © Gio Barto/tips images/age fotostock; 23R, © Lukáš Hejtman/Shutterstock; 24, © Spectrum Photofile Inc.; 25, © Dave Porter/Alamy; 26L, © AF archive/ Alamy; 26R, © ITAR-TASS/Karo-Film Press Service/Newscom; 27, © Hadas Dembo/Taxi/Getty Images; 28, © Utekhina Anna/Shutterstock; 29T, © Eric Isselée/Shutterstock; 29B, © Alice Van Kempen/Animal-Photography; 31, © Julia Remezova/Shutterstock.

Publisher: Kenn Goin
Editorial Director: Adam Siegel
Creative Director: Spencer Brinker
Design: Dawn Beard Creative
Cover Design: Dawn Beard Creative and Kim Jones
Photo Researcher: Mary Fran Loftus

Library of Congress Cataloging-in-Publication Data

Bluemel Oldfield, Dawn.
  Newfoundland : water rescuer / by Dawn Bluemel Oldfield ; Consultant, Jim Bricknell.
     p. cm. — (Big dogs rule)
  Includes bibliographical references and index.
  ISBN-13: 978-1-61772-296-7 (library binding)
  ISBN-10: 1-61772-296-0 (library binding)
  1. Newfoundland dog—Juvenile literature. I. Title.
  SF429.N4B58 2012
  636.73—dc23
                    2011019413

For more information, write to Bearport Publishing Company, Inc., 45 West 21st Street, Suite 3B, New York, New York 10010. Printed in the United States of America in North Mankato, Minnesota.

072011
042711CGF

10 9 8 7 6 5 4 3 2 1

Contents

Lifeguard Dog

On a summer day in 2007, Bilbo was **patrolling** the beach at Sennen Cove in Cornwall, England. The big Newfoundland watched the water closely. He knew the large, rolling waves of the Atlantic Ocean were dangerous. They could easily drag swimmers below the **surface** and drown them.

On duty, Bilbo ▶ wears a lifeguard vest with swimming safety messages written on it.

Suddenly, Bilbo saw Lein Snippe start to enter the water to swim. The huge dog, weighing almost 200 pounds (91 kg), tried to block her path. When Lein went in anyway, Bilbo raced into the ocean and swam in front of her.

Lein realized that Bilbo was warning her not to swim there. She said that it was as if he were saying to her, "It's too dangerous—don't go in." Not wanting to risk her life, Lein quickly left the water. Once again, Bilbo's lifesaving actions showed why Newfoundlands have earned the **breed** the nickname of "lifeguard dog."

Bilbo to the rescue

Bilbo became so popular while working at Sennen Cove that a book was written about him. It's called *The True Story of Bilbo: The Surf Lifeguard Dog.*

Built for the Job

Newfoundlands such as Bilbo have worked for many years on beaches in Britain, France, and Italy. What makes members of the breed such good lifeguards? For one thing, their bodies are perfect for the job. The giant dogs have strong muscles that allow them to move easily in the water. They can also swim far without getting out of breath because their large **lungs** hold lots of air.

▲ Lifeguard Steve Jamieson (above), Bilbo's owner, said his quick-thinking Newfoundland has saved at least three lives while working at the beach.

A Newfoundland's two layers of fur also help it work as a lifeguard. The thick and oily outer **coat** is waterproof, keeping the dog's skin dry in the cold ocean. The soft undercoat helps keep the dog's body warm. A Newfoundland also has **webbed** paws similar to a duck's feet. The extra skin between the toes helps the dog quickly push its body through the water. In addition, the animal uses its long, strong tail to change direction as it swims.

Newfoundlands do not paddle in the water the way most other dogs do. Instead, they move their legs down and out, giving them a powerful swimming **stroke**.

▲ **These Newfoundlands work as lifeguards to help keep swimmers in Italy safe.**

Trained for Trouble

Newfoundlands have the perfect bodies for water rescues. However, these dogs—also called Newfies or Newfs—must be carefully trained to work as lifeguards. They learn to swim around a person in trouble while pulling a **rescue float** that's attached to their bodies. Once the swimmer grabs the float, the dog pulls the person to safety.

▲ **This painting shows a Newfie pulling a life preserver in order to rescue a swimmer in trouble.**

If a swimmer is **unconscious**, the Newf is taught to gently grab the person's upper arm with its mouth. The dog then forces the victim to roll onto his or her back. Doing this keeps the person's face out of the water so that he or she does not drown. Finally, the Newf pulls the victim to land.

Newfoundlands have a **natural** desire to rescue people in need. Even without being trained, they can sense when swimmers are in danger of drowning.

▲ **This Newf gently grabs hold of a person's hand as he brings the swimmer to safety.**

Greater and Lesser

Newfoundlands are famous for their brave water rescues. Long ago, however, they were known for doing other jobs as well. The dogs originally came from Newfoundland, a large island off the eastern coast of Canada. In the 1700s, people on the island used two types of working dogs—one large and one medium-size.

ICELAND

Newfoundland

Atlantic Ocean

Pacific Ocean

Newfoundland dogs were named after the island in Canada that they came from.

Canada has issued postage stamps that honor its **native** dog.

Canada 37

Newfoundland • Terre-neuve

The large dogs with long, furry coats were called greater Newfoundlands. The medium-size dogs with smooth coats were called lesser Newfoundlands. Fishermen used both kinds of dogs to **haul** their fishing equipment. Other people used greater Newfoundlands to pull wagons filled with milk, wood, or other items. Over time, the greater Newfoundland came to be known simply as the Newfoundland. The lesser Newfoundland developed into a breed that is today called the Labrador **retriever**.

◀ **A Newfie pulling a wagon**

Labrador retrievers also ▶
work as lifeguard dogs.

Fishy Work

Of all their jobs, Newfies worked hardest in Newfoundland's busy fishing **industry**. In the ocean, they spread out large nets that workers used to catch fish. Once the nets were full, the dogs pulled them back to the fishing boats. Later, the Newfs were **hitched** to wagons to haul the fishermen's catch into town.

▲ **These fishermen in Canada are moving a heavy net full of fish. Newfoundlands used to help with this kind of work.**

Newfs were also kept on ships in case of emergencies. Sometimes, fishing boats would get tossed in the stormy sea. The waters were often too rough for the **stranded** ship to make it safely to **shore**. To help out, one end of a **lifeline** was tied to the boat and a Newfie would swim to shore with the other end in its mouth. A person on land would tie this end to a **dock**. Workers onboard the ship would then hold on to the line and pull themselves to land.

Besides pulling fishing nets and wagons, Newfoundlands also retrieved any equipment that accidentally fell off the fishing boats.

▲ **A Newfoundland pulling a ship's lifeline to shore**

Spreading Out

For years, Newfoundlands lived only on their home island in Canada. Then, in the early 1800s, English explorers came to the area. They were impressed by the large working dogs they saw there. They brought Newfies back to England, where the big dogs were **bred**. Soon, Newfoundlands were brought to other places, including the United States.

Most Newfoundlands in the world today can be traced back to the dogs that were bred in England.

▲ The English artist Sir Edwin Henry Landseer (1802–1873) made many paintings, such as this one, of black and white Newfoundlands. Today, black and white Newfoundlands are often called Landseer Newfoundlands.

In 1804, a Newfoundland named Seaman traveled with Meriwether Lewis and William Clark as they explored the American northwest. Seaman was an important part of the team. The dog helped Lewis and Clark hunt animals. He also guarded the camp at night, barking if wild animals, such as bears and buffalo, came near.

▲ **This painting by Anne Mainman is titled *Lewis and Clark's Newfoundland Seaman*.**

◄ **This statue of Lewis and Clark with their dog Seaman can be seen in Sioux City, Iowa.**

That's Big!

The **American Kennel Club** (AKC) is an organization that keeps records of the different kinds of dogs bred in the United States. For each breed of dog, the AKC writes a **standard**. This detailed description explains how the **ideal** dog of the breed should look and behave.

▼ **Newfoundlands that meet the AKC standard are able to enter and win awards at dog shows.**

The AKC standard for the Newfoundland describes the breed as "a large dog." How large is large? According to the AKC, the average male Newfoundland is 28 inches (71 cm) tall at the shoulder. The female is 26 inches (66 cm) tall. Males weigh from 130 to 150 pounds (59 to 68 kg). Females weigh from 100 to 120 pounds (45 to 54 kg).

A Newfoundland named Boomer is one of the biggest dogs in the world. He is 36 inches (91 cm) tall from paw to shoulder, and stretches seven feet (2 m) from his nose to the tip of his tail!

▼ **Boomer weighs 180 pounds (82 kg)—as much as a washing machine!**

Keeping Busy

The AKC standard describes the Newfoundland as a "**multipurpose** dog." This means that these working dogs can perform many kinds of jobs. Some such as Bilbo rescue swimmers from dangerous waters. In Newfoundland, many Newfs are still used to pull wagons and carry heavy loads on their backs.

In Italy, Newfoundlands are taught to jump from a helicopter in order to rescue struggling swimmers in the ocean.

Because Newfoundlands are loving and gentle animals, they also work well as **therapy dogs**. They visit children's hospitals and nursing homes, where patients like to pet and hug the huge, furry dogs. Other Newfies make good **service dogs**. They are trained to help **disabled** people, such as individuals in wheelchairs.

◀ Newfies can bring both help and happiness to people who are sick or lonely.

▼ Connie, a Newfie that works as a service dog, helps out her owner by putting dirty laundry into a washing machine—and then switching the machine on with her paw.

Newfoundlands are able to assist people in many ways because of their great size and strength. They can be taught to open doors and even to lift up and carry someone who has fallen.

Popular Pets

Newfoundlands are more than just working dogs. They're also popular household pets. Nicknamed "gentle giants," these big creatures have a sweet, friendly nature. They love to play with people, especially children. A Newf might put a toy in its mouth and then encourage family members to join in a game of chase!

Newfoundlands can live indoors. However, the big dogs also need an outdoor area where they can run and play during the day.

Newfies are also popular pets because they are calm and patient. They are gentle with other animals and with visitors to the home. However, Newfs are also quick to sense danger. They are loyal and **protective** of family members. Their great size and strength—along with their deep, loud bark—make them excellent watchdogs.

▲ The Newfoundland has been called "the nanny dog" because it is so good with children.

Important Tips

To keep a Newfie healthy and happy, people who are thinking about getting one need to learn about the breed's special needs. For example, Newfoundlands like to play outdoors. However, their thick, heavy coats can cause them to become too hot on a sunny day. As a result, owners need to make sure the dogs stay in the shade to keep cool. In addition, they should give the dogs an extra bowl of water to lap up in the heat.

Newfies are easy to train, especially when they are young. Owners should remain calm yet firm when teaching the dog how to behave.

▲ **An owner training her Newfoundland to lie down**

Owners also need to regularly **groom** their Newfies. The dogs have long, thick hair that picks up dirt and **mats** easily. To stay clean and shiny, a Newfoundland's coat must be brushed at least once a week. Owners should also know that Newfies can be messy dogs. They tend to drool, especially after drinking. To keep their home clean, owners should be ready to wipe the wetness off furniture and floors.

◄ **Newfies love to be with people, and can quickly grow bored if left alone.**

▲ **People who don't like a dog that drools should think twice before getting a Newfoundland.**

New Newfs

Newfoundlands grow to be large dogs, yet they start out very small. When they are born, Newfies weigh only about one pound (.5 kg). The furry creatures look like tiny bear cubs. By the age of eight weeks, however, the pups have grown to 15 pounds (6.8 kg). That's the same weight as a heavy bowling ball!

A **litter** of Newfoundlands usually has six to ten puppies.

When Newfies are first born, they get all the food they need by drinking milk from their mother's body.

After four months, a baby Newf is big enough to start swimming in a pool. It quickly learns to retrieve small items such as sticks, balls, or shoes from the water. Usually, the dog reaches its full size after one year. By then, it weighs around 130 pounds (59 kg)—more than some adults weigh!

▲ **Even as puppies, Newfoundlands love the water.**

Big Dogs, Big Hearts

While Newfoundlands make wonderful working dogs and pets, the lovable canines have also become well known in another way. They are featured in many popular books and movies. In the *Harry Potter* books, the character of Sirius Black is able to turn from human to dog and back again using his magic powers. In the *Harry Potter* movies, a black Newfoundland plays the role of Sirius Black when he is a dog.

In the 2005 movie *Must Love Dogs*, one of the main characters is a Newfoundland dog. Two six-month-old Newfie pups shared the job of acting the role in the film.

Sirius Black appears as ▶ both a dog and as a human (as shown here on the left) in the *Harry Potter* books and movies.

Another famous **fictional** Newfoundland is Nana, the "nurse dog" in the 1904 play *Peter Pan* by J. M. Barrie. Her character was based on the author's real-life Newfoundland named Luath. As the nanny for the Darling family in *Peter Pan*, Nana takes care of the children.

Loving and loyal Newfoundlands such as Nana don't exist just in movies and plays, however. As any Newf owner in real life will tell you, the big dogs show their families just how big their hearts are every day.

Newfoundlands at a Glance

Weight:	Male: 130–150 pounds (59–68 kg) Female: 100–120 pounds (45–54 kg)
Height at Shoulder:	Male: 28 inches (71 cm) Female: 26 inches (66 cm)
Coat Hair:	Long, stiff, oily outer coat; soft, thick hair underneath
Colors:	Solid black, brown, or gray; some are white with black, brown, or gray markings
Country of Origin:	The Canadian island of Newfoundland
Life Span:	About ten years
Personality:	Calm, gentle, brave, hardworking, loyal, protective, intelligent, playful

Best in Show

What makes a great Newfoundland? Every owner knows that his or her dog is special. Judges in dog shows, however, look very carefully at a Newfoundland's appearance and behavior. Here are some of the things they look for:

head is large and wide

back is strong, wide, and level

tail is strong; hangs straight or slightly curved when the dog Is relaxed

legs are straight and parallel

outer coat is flat, stiff, and medium-long; undercoat is soft and thick

Behavior: calm, friendly, gentle, intelligent, alert

Glossary

American Kennel Club (uh-MER-i-kuhn KEN-uhl KLUHB) a national organization that is involved with many activities having to do with dogs, including collecting information about dog breeds and setting rules for dog shows

bred (BRED) raised

breed (BREED) a kind of dog

coat (KOHT) the hair or fur on an animal

disabled (diss-AY-buhld) unable to do certain things due to an injury or illness

dock (DOK) a landing area where ships load and unload goods

fictional (FIK-shuh-nuhl) not true or real; made-up

groom (GROOM) to brush and clean

haul (HAWL) to pull

hitched (HICHT) fastened to something with a rope or other item

ideal (eye-DEE-uhl) the perfect example of something

industry (IN-duh-stree) a type of business

lifeline (LIFE-line) a rope used to rescue someone who is drowning

litter (LIT-ur) a group of baby animals, such as puppies or kittens, that are born to the same mother at the same time

lungs (LUHNGZ) parts of the body in a person's or an animal's chest that are used for breathing

mats (MATS) becomes a thick, tangled mass

multipurpose (*muhl*-tee-PUR-puhss) having more than one use

native (NAY-tiv) belonging to a particular place because of where one was born

natural (NACH-ur-uhl) present from birth rather than having been learned

patrolling (puh-TROHL-ing) walking or traveling around an area to protect it or to keep watch on people

protective (pruh-TEK-tiv) guarding or keeping something safe from harm

rescue float (RESS-kyoo FLOHT) a device used to pull a drowning swimmer back to land

retriever (ri-TREE-vur) any of several breeds of dogs that are trained to find and bring back animals shot by hunters

service dogs (SUR-viss DAWGZ) dogs that are trained to help disabled people, such as those in wheelchairs

shore (SHOR) land along the edge of a body of water such as an ocean or lake

standard (STAN-durd) a description of the "perfect" dog in each breed

stranded (STRAN-did) left helpless in a strange or dangerous place

stroke (STROHK) a way of moving when swimming

surface (SUR-fiss) the top or outermost layer of something

therapy dogs (THER-uh-pee DAWGZ) dogs that visit places such as hospitals to cheer up people and make them feel more comfortable

unconscious (uhn-KON-shuhss) not awake; not able to see, feel, or think

webbed (WEBD) having toes connected by skin that helps an animal swim

Bibliography

Barlowe, Angela. *Newfoundland: A Comprehensive Guide to Owning and Caring for Your Dog.* Allenhurst, NJ: Kennel Club Books (2003).

Hynes, Bruce. *The Noble Newfoundland Dog.* Halifax, Nova Scotia: Nimbus (2005).

Kosloff, Joanna. *Newfoundlands (A Complete Pet Owner's Manual).* Hauppauge, NY: Barron's Educational Series (2006).

Riley, Jo Ann. *The Newfoundland: Gentle Giant.* Loveland, CO: Alpine Blue Ribbon Books (2004).

Read More

Landau, Elaine. *Newfoundlands Are the Best! (The Best Dogs Ever).* Minneapolis, MN: Lerner (2011).

Wheeler, Jill C. *Newfoundlands.* Edina, MN: ABDO Publishing (2010).

Wilcox, Charlotte. *The Newfoundland.* Mankato, MN: Capstone (1999).

Learn More Online

To learn more about Newfoundlands, visit
www.bearportpublishing.com/BigDogsRule

Index

About the Author

Dawn Bluemel Oldfield is a freelance writer. She and her husband live in Prosper, Texas. They love animals and share their home with two fabulous cats and one terrific dog, a Siberian husky named McKenna.